Contents

Some words are shown in bold, **like this**. You can find them in a glossary on page 23.

Marvellous meerkats

Meerkats live in deserts in Africa. They live in large groups called **mobs**.

When there are many things to count, we can put them into groups to make the counting go faster. Let's count a mob of meerkats!

̄oun_ing in ̄s

Start with two meerkat **pups**.

Add two more.

$$2 + 2 = 4$$

Two plus two is four. There are **double** the meerkat pups.

Here are two more meerkat pups!
Let's add them on.

There are two meerkats in each group.
There are three groups of two. Add the
groups together.

$$2 + 2 + 2 = 6$$

There are six meerkats in all.

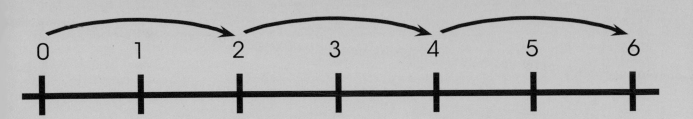

When we add the same numbers together, we can also use **multiples** to find the answer.

How many meerkats are in this **mob**?

Count in **multiples** of two to find out!

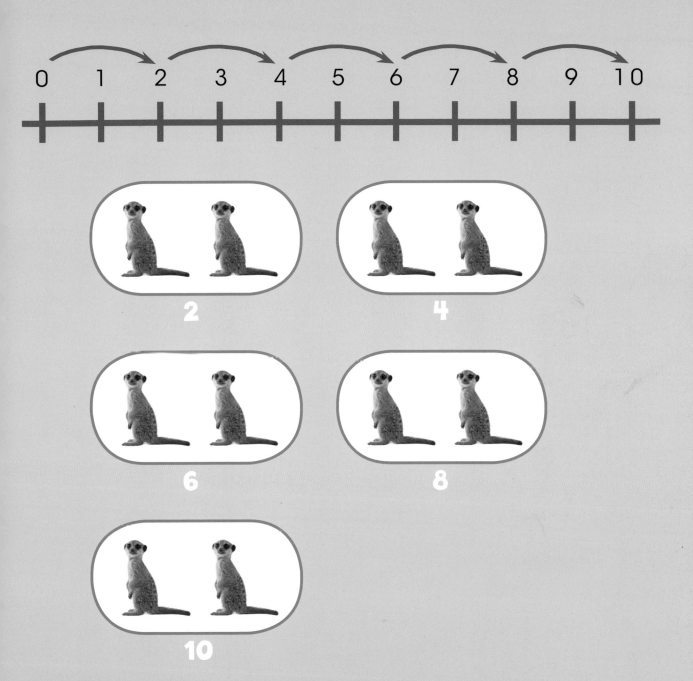

There are ten meerkats in the mob.

Meerkats get hungry! This meerkat is eating a scorpion.

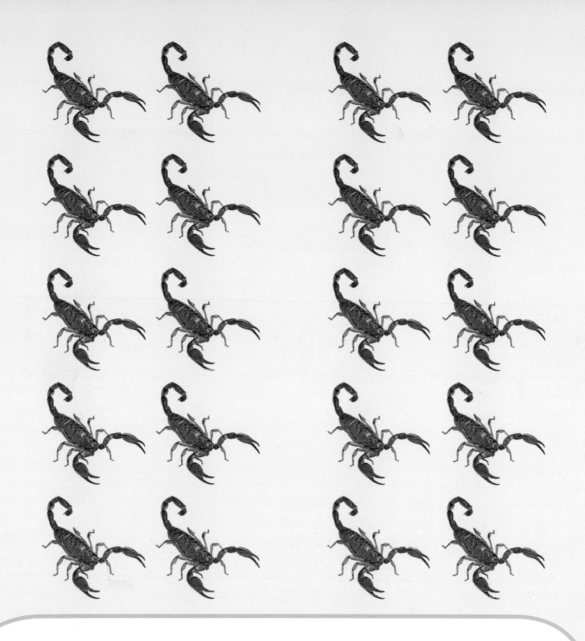

Look at all these scorpions! Let's use **multiples** to find out how many there are.

We can count in **multiples** of two.

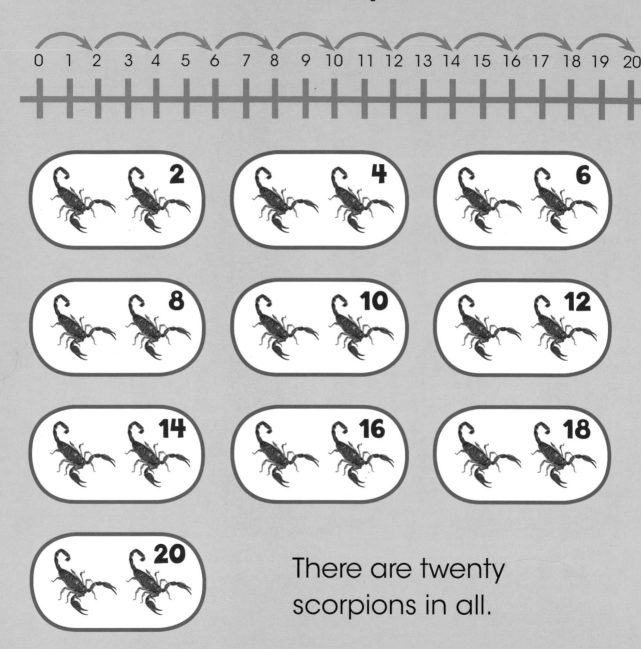

There are twenty scorpions in all.

14

Counting in 5s

We can also count in multiples of five!

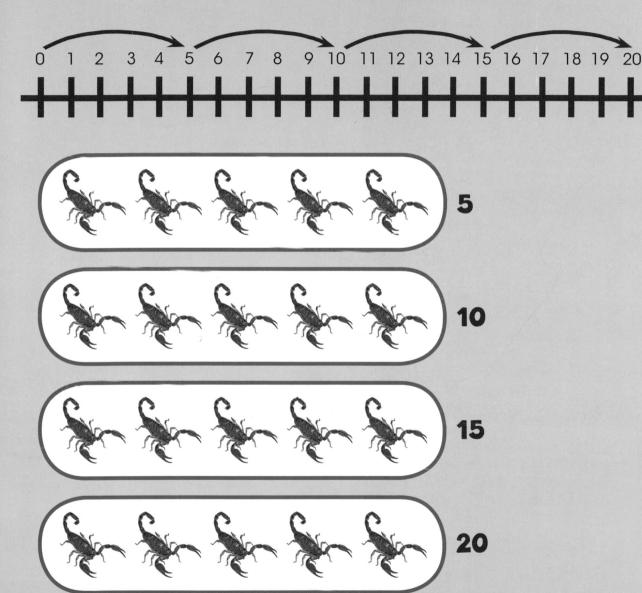

There are plenty of scorpions for lunch!

There can be a lot of meerkats in one **mob**. Look at all these meerkats! It would take a long time to count each one. Counting in **multiples** is faster!

Put the meerkats in groups of five. Count in 5s to find out how many there are altogether.

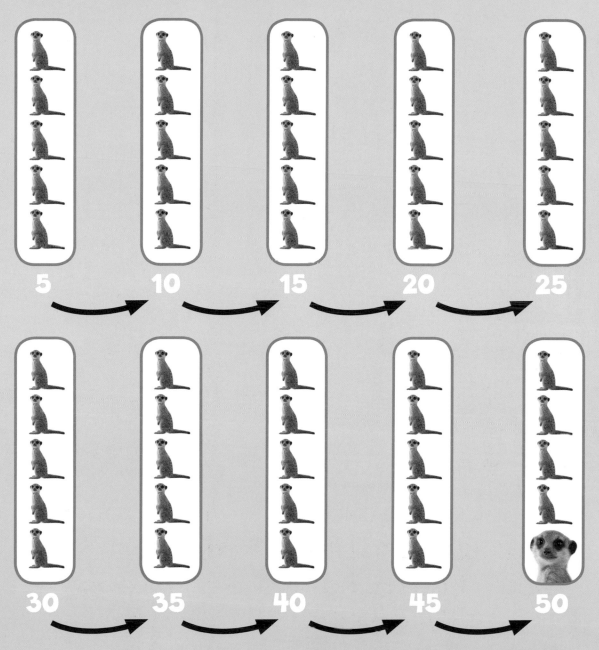

5   10   15   20   25

30   35   40   45   50

There are fifty meerkats in all!

Counting in 10s

We can also count in **multiples** of ten. Look at the pattern. All the numbers end in zero.

10 ten

20 twenty

30 thirty

40 forty

50 fifty

60 sixty

70 seventy

80 eighty

90 ninety

100 one hundred

Now put the meerkats in groups of ten and use multiples to count to fifty.

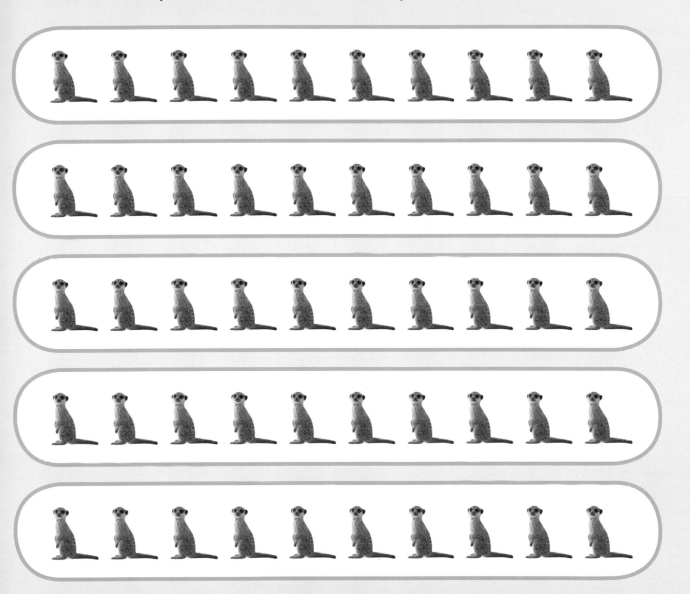

Using multiples of ten is even faster than using multiples of five!

19

Hundred charts

This hundred chart shows numbers in a pattern. It can help you to count using **multiples** of five and ten.

1	2	3	4	5	6	7	8	9	10
11	12	13	14	15	16	17	18	19	20
21	22	23	24	25	26	27	28	29	30
31	32	33	34	35	36	37	38	39	40
41	42	43	44	45	46	47	48	49	50
51	52	53	54	55	56	57	58	59	60
61	62	63	64	65	66	67	68	69	70
71	72	73	74	75	76	77	78	79	80
81	82	83	84	85	86	87	88	89	90
91	92	93	94	95	96	97	98	99	100

Look! There are many meerkats!

How many are there? Count in
multiples of ten to find out.

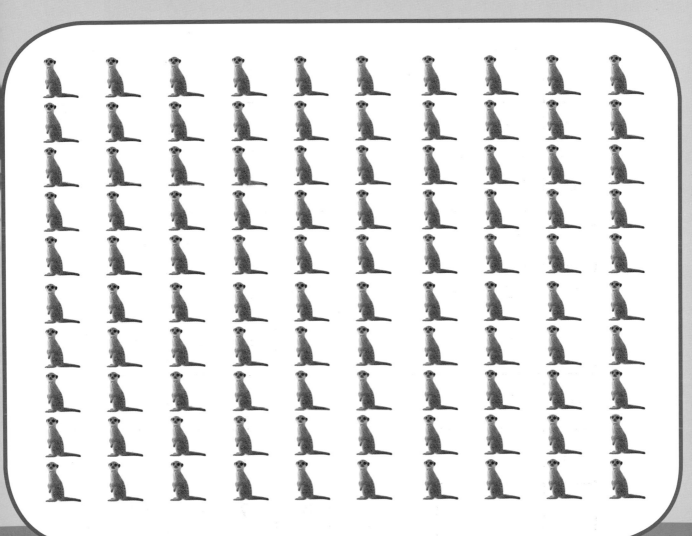

Answer on page 22.

Meerkat facts

- Meerkats often live in groups of about 20, but there can be 50 or more meerkats in a **mob**.

- Meerkats stand up tall to look out for danger. One member of the group is always watching out for enemies.

- Meerkats are not cats. They are members of the mongoose family.

- Meerkats mostly eat insects, but they also eat scorpions, lizards, and plants.

There are 100 meerkats!

Answer

uths glossary

double to have twice as much of something

multiples groups of numbers that go up by the same amount each time

For example:
    2, 4, 6, 8, and 10 are multiples of 2
    5, 10, 15, 20, and 25 are multiples of 5
    10, 20, 30, 40, and 50 are multiples of 10

eerkat glossary

mob a group of meerkats

pup a young meerkat

Index